Eye on the Wild

Eye on the Wild

A Story about Ansel Adams

by Julie Dunlap
illustrations by Kerry Maguire

A Carolrhoda Creative Minds Book

Carolrhoda Books, Inc./Minneapolis

To my son, Nathan Vogel, who loves music and wild places—J.D.

This book is available in two editions:
Library binding by Carolrhoda Books, Inc.
Soft cover by First Avenue Editions
c/o The Lerner Group
241 First Avenue North
Minneapolis, Minnesota 55401

Library of Congress Cataloging-in-Publication Data

Dunlap, Julie.
    Eye on the wild : a story about Ansel Adams / by Julie Dunlap ;
illustrated by Kerry Maguire.
      p. cm. — (A Carolrhoda creative minds book)
    Includes bibliographical references.
    ISBN 0-87614-944-1 (lib. bdg.)
    ISBN 0-87614-966-2 (pbk.)
    1. Adams, Ansel, 1902– —Juvenile literature. 2. Photographers—
United States—Biography—Juvenile literature. [1. Adams, Ansel, 1902– .
2. Photographers.] I. Maguire, Kerry, ill. II. Title. III. Series.
TR140.A3D86   1995
770′.92—dc20
[B]   94-42172
                                                    CIP
                                                      AC

Manufactured in the United States of America
1 2 3 4 5 6 – MA – 00 99 98 97 96 95

Table of Contents

Golden Gate　　　　　　　　　7

Music and Mountains　　　　　17

The Range of Light　　　　　27

Beautiful beyond Words　　　40

The American Earth　　　　　51

Afterword　　　　　　　　　62

Bibliography　　　　　　　　63

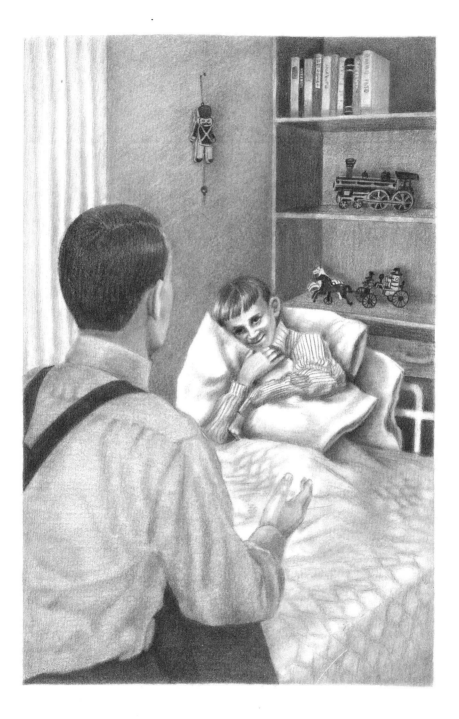

① Golden Gate

Twelve-year-old Ansel lay in his dark bedroom, struggling not to scratch the bumpy red rash on his arms. Trapped in bed with the measles! The doctor had ordered him to rest for two weeks with the shades down to protect his eyes. Ansel couldn't even look out his window at the ships sailing through the Golden Gate into San Francisco Bay.

One morning, the restless patient noticed fuzzy images flickering on the ceiling. Shafts of light passing through tiny holes above one window shade were projecting pictures of someone outside. How were the pictures being made? Ansel wondered. He puzzled over the mystery all day.

By the time his father came home from work, Ansel was bursting with questions. Charles Adams smiled at his only child's hungry mind. The holes above the shade work like pin-hole cameras, Charles explained.

Charles opened his box camera and clicked the shutter. A tiny hole opened up. Charles showed his son how light rays bounce off an object in front of the camera and pass through the hole to project a picture inside the box. If the camera held light-sensitive film, Charles said, the image would be recorded on it. Ansel leaned happily against his pillows, snapping the shutter and studying the light.

Ever since Ansel had been born, on February 20, 1902, Charles Adams had hoped his son would share his passion for science and nature. Charles had wanted to be an astronomer, but his father had insisted he take over the family lumber business. The job had brought him wealth. He had built a fine home on the Pacific Ocean outside of San Francisco and hired a nanny to help his wife, Olive, look after their lively baby. But Charles preferred studying the stars to managing lumber mills.

At an early age, Ansel had shown he shared his father's curious nature. On April 18, 1906, a violent earthquake awakened the Adams household. Four-year-old Ansel's bed careened across his room, and the chimney snapped off the roof. When the roaring and shaking stopped, Ansel's terrified mother carried him downstairs to check the damage.

Shattered china and bricks littered the floor,

mixed with smashed jars of preserves. Instead of being frightened, little Ansel was fascinated. Seeing the scattered gears of a broken grandfather clock, he shouted cheerfully, "Now I can play with the clockworks!"

That same morning, an aftershock flung Ansel against a wall, breaking his nose. Throughout nearby San Francisco, hundreds died, and thousands lost their homes and businesses in the fires that followed the quake. Ansel's family stood by their window in the evening, watching the eerie glow of the burning city.

The earthquake was only one of the disasters Ansel's family then faced. Between 1897 and 1907, three of their lumber mills burned and twenty-seven ships were lost at sea. The Adams fortune was crumbling.

By 1908 Olive's father also had lost his money in bad investments. Grandfather Bray and his other daughter, Ansel's aunt Mary, had to move in with the Adamses. Olive's spirits sank as money grew scarce, but Charles was determined to hold the family together. He found a job in an insurance office and sent his son off to school.

Though bright and energetic, Ansel was a poor student. Schoolwork seemed pointless. He couldn't see a reason to memorize strings of dull facts—like which states border Nebraska—so he refused to learn. Classmates considered the skinny, dark-eyed boy shy and "odd." They left him alone to daydream. He dreamed most about exploring the sand dunes around his house. How could he sit still in class when he longed to be outside?

Whenever he could escape from school, Ansel loved to run. By age nine, he was rushing outside on Saturdays at dawn, down Lobos Creek to the rocky Pacific coast. In the gray mist, mournful foghorns warned ships' captains to be careful. But Ansel climbed the slippery cliffs, clinging by his fingertips.

At Baker Beach, he listened to the cries of seagulls while collecting driftwood at the tideline. And when the sun began to burn through the fog, Ansel crouched on the cold sand, watching light shimmering on the waves.

But the sand dunes around Ansel's house were gradually disappearing. San Francisco was growing quickly, and the rolling dunes were being scraped flat to make house lots. The Adamses' new neighbors liked neat yards and straight streets, but Ansel and his father missed the wildflowers and scrubby sea grass. As Ansel grew, he had to run farther and farther on Saturdays to find wild places to play.

Returning to school each Monday was always a trial. At age twelve, the year he figured out how cameras work, Ansel spent hours investigating his father's telescope and other complicated devices at home. But in class, he simply could not stop fidgeting. Teachers called him a troublemaker, and more than once the principal sent him home.

His parents, however, were confident about Ansel's abilities. They finally decided to have him study at home. Charles taught him French and algebra, and a minister tutored him in Greek. In his free time, he read classic books of literature. Home teaching sparked Ansel's curiosity, although he still wouldn't stick with anything that bored him.

For fun, Ansel started picking out tunes on an old piano. His parents were impressed (and surprised) by his musical talent. "Four months ago he didn't know a note," Charles wrote his sister, but now, "he can read almost anything put before him at sight."

A neighbor who taught piano agreed that Ansel had an extraordinary gift. But he must be properly trained, Marie Butler insisted. Miss Butler drilled Ansel on scales and finger exercises, demanding perfection.

Ansel loved the beautiful, precise sounds he learned to make. The tough piano training gave him self-discipline. Still, it was hard to keep practicing when a sea breeze drifted through the window.

In 1915 Charles found an unusual way to educate Ansel. San Francisco was hosting the Panama-Pacific World's Fair to celebrate the opening of the Panama Canal, and Charles gave his son a year's pass to the fair.

Ansel spent hours each day wandering through grand exhibits from around the world. He tinkered with the new inventions on display, questioned exhibitors, ate ice cream, and, of course, rode the roller coaster. In the Palace of Fine Arts, Ansel got his first look at modern paintings and sculpture.

One day, while wandering the fairgrounds, Ansel found a piano in a lounge where sightseers rested. He returned often to play, and every time, more visitors gathered to listen. When Charles dropped by one afternoon, he proudly observed there was standing room only.

The next April, Ansel was sick in bed with a cold when his aunt Mary gave him an old book to help pass the time. *In the Heart of the Sierras,* published in 1886, was written to encourage hardy tourists to visit Yosemite Valley.

The valley, high in the mountains east of San Francisco, had been made a California state park in 1864 to save its lush scenery. But the park protected only the valley, not the surrounding high country. By the 1880s, thousands of sheep were trampling grass in the high meadows, and loggers were chopping down acres of mountain sugar pines.

A few people, called preservationists, believed that certain places of great beauty, such as the dramatic rocky rim above Yosemite Valley, should be protected from change. John Muir was the preservationists' strongest spokesman. He declared that people needed the High Sierra's natural beauty as much as they needed wool or logs. He thought the land above the valley would be best protected as a national park, like Yellowstone (established in 1872).

In 1890, after years of struggle by Muir and his followers, 1,500 square miles of high country were protected as Yosemite National Park. And in 1905, the valley, too, became part of the national park.

Ansel read and reread *In the Heart of the Sierras*. Looking at the book's dim black-and-white photographs, he imagined perching on a granite cliff, listening to a roaring waterfall. He must see this magical place! On the family's next vacation, Ansel pleaded with his parents, could they go to Yosemite?

After a month of waiting, Ansel and his family crowded into a hot car of the Yosemite Valley Railroad. At the town of El Portal, they boarded an open bus headed up a twisting gravel road that climbed into the cool Sierra. At last, Yosemite Valley appeared before them: the green Merced River, flowering azaleas, towering cliffs, gleaming waterfalls. Ansel was dazzled.

Scattered around the valley floor were hotels, cabins, tents, a bakery, and other stores. The Adams family decided to stay in a large campground called Camp Curry. Ansel was so worn out by the day's excitement that he fell asleep instantly.

In the next morning's cold air, Ansel's parents presented him with his first camera. The Kodak Box Brownie was simple and small enough to take exploring. Though other visitors stuck to the trails, Ansel dashed through meadows, climbed rocks, and played along the river as he snapped photographs.

To get a good picture of a famous peak called Half Dome, he climbed a rotting tree stump. The stump crumbled, pitching Ansel into the dirt. But on the way down, he clicked the shutter. Ansel Adams's first photograph of Half Dome was taken upside down.

②
Music and Mountains

After his Yosemite vacation, Ansel had collected his snapshots into a diary of his trip. The fun of taking pictures was growing into a fascination with photography. To learn more, fifteen-year-old Ansel took a summer job at a neighbor's photofinishing business. Photography was such a popular hobby in 1917 that there were hundreds of rolls of film to develop each day in Frank Dittman's basement darkroom.

Thirty-six rolls at a time were dipped for five minutes in a deep tank of developing chemicals. Next, the film was rinsed and then swished for one minute in the fixing bath. Another rinse and the negatives were ready to dry—and printmaking could begin. Light shining through the negatives onto light-sensitive paper exposed the prints. Ansel loved to experiment with the length of light exposure needed to make the best pictures.

As they made prints, the darkroom workers talked and joked. Ansel told so many stories about his Yosemite adventures that the others nicknamed him Ansel "Yosemite" Adams.

Despite Ansel's enjoyment of photography, playing piano was what he took most seriously. In 1918 he graduated to a new piano teacher, Frederick Zech. Never had Ansel studied so hard. Each day, said Mr. Zech, Ansel should play an hour of finger exercises, an hour of Bach, an hour of Beethoven, and two hours of other composers. Ansel practiced so much that sometimes he bruised his fingertips.

Playing scales up and down felt like climbing hills and valleys to Ansel. As his fingers grew more nimble, his spirits soared. Ansel began to dream of a career as a concert pianist. It would be hard, he knew, for his father to pay for a long musical education. But Charles Adams recognized his son's gift and vowed that Ansel could follow the career he chose.

But Yosemite Adams's mind still wandered at times. He loved California's wilds. After two family trips to Yosemite, Ansel headed for the valley without his parents in May 1918. Watching over him was a family friend and retired engineer, Francis Holman, who studied birds in the Sierra each summer.

"Uncle Frank" took Ansel on his first back-country camping trips, teaching him how to build a campfire, cook flapjacks, catch trout, manage pack burros, and find smooth ground to sleep on. Unfortunately, it was usually too dark at the end of a day's hike to see if there were any ants' nests under the sleeping bags. The campers often awoke squirming in the frigid darkness, covered with the biting insects.

To Ansel, that summer's highlights were dangerous climbs up Half Dome and other peaks. Tied together with window-sash cord, Uncle Frank and Ansel inched up slopes of polished granite and leaped over rocks and gullies. One slip on a patch of ice could have meant a fall to their deaths (though Ansel's letters home assured his mother that the trips were "perfectly safe"). Exhausted by a long climb, they would rest on a narrow ledge, munching raisins and sipping cold water from a melting snowbank. After his winter of rigid piano practice, the freedom of Yosemite was delicious.

Another park trip in 1919 inspired Ansel to apply for work there the next summer as caretaker of the LeConte Memorial Lodge. The lodge was the local headquarters for the Sierra Club, a small group of preservationists founded by John Muir in 1892.

Dedicated to teaching people about the Sierra Nevada, the club published a magazine, *The Sierra Club Bulletin,* led hiking trips, and helped build hiking trails in the mountains. Sierra Club members, Muir hoped, would work together "to do something for wildness and make the mountains glad."

Ansel joined the Sierra Club in 1919 and became caretaker of the LeConte Lodge in 1920. To help visitors enjoy Yosemite National Park, the lodge housed small collections of maps, pressed flowers, and books on mountain climbing. Ansel's duties were to watch over the collections and answer visitors' questions while keeping a welcoming fire burning in the huge fireplace. Once a week, he also led a few hikers on the long trek up to the valley rim.

The job left him plenty of free time to explore on his own. The lanky teenager with the camera and the crooked nose (from the earthquake accident) became a familiar sight around the park. For his high-country trips with Uncle Frank, Ansel bought his own pack burro, Mistletoe. They tramped through pine and fir forests to Lake Merced, miles from crowded Yosemite Valley. One morning, Ansel scaled a towering rock to watch the sun rise. Light sparkled on rugged, unnamed mountains. Here, Ansel thought, is true wilderness.

An increasingly serious musician, Ansel knew he should not spend summers exploring without practicing. In 1921 he discovered a piano in Yosemite Village at Best's Studio. Harry Best, a painter who sold souvenirs at his shop, invited Ansel to play there anytime. More than the piano drew Ansel to Best's— there was also Harry's seventeen-year-old daughter. A talented singer and brave climber, Virginia Best loved music and mountains as much as Ansel did. By the next summer, Ansel wrote to his parents that he was in love.

At home in San Francisco that fall, Ansel pushed himself to work harder than ever. He needed to be earning a living before he and Virginia could marry. So besides hours of practice and lessons, he taught a few piano students. Most of his friends were musicians too, including violinist Cedric Wright. Cedric hosted noisy parties where Ansel's sense of humor shined. The once-shy boy joked and clowned, even playing wrong notes on the piano to amuse his friends.

Though devoted to his music, he studied artistic photography on the side. After photography was invented in the early 1800s, most photographers simply tried to record the people and places they saw. Few treated photography as an art. How could a mechanical device like a camera express an artist's feelings? people asked. But as photographic techniques improved, photographers gained more control over how their pictures looked. Some began to believe that photographs could be creative, even fine art.

In the early 1900s, artistic photographers created the "pictorial" style of photography. They used special lenses, brushwork, and chemicals to make fuzzy prints that looked like paintings or charcoal drawings. Although few art museums would show the photographs, photographers sponsored their own exhibits to display their pictorial prints.

These techniques fascinated Ansel. He experimented eagerly with lenses, printing papers, and a new bromoil printing process. As with the piano, he practiced and practiced to perfect his craft. He wrote to Virginia about his success. He was even earning money from his photos. A mounted Ansel Adams print sold in 1923 for $2.50.

In 1924 and 1925, Ansel spent his summers with Sierra Club friends, exploring and photographing Kings Canyon south of Yosemite in the Sierra Nevada. Along with pots, a sleeping bag, and tinned meats, his burro's pack held the tools of an expert photographer: a bulky view camera, lenses, filters, and coated glass plates (used instead of film to make finer pictures). In his hand, Ansel carried the wooden tripod needed to support the heavy equipment. The wilderness trips and his growing photographic skill delighted Ansel. But he was also worried. Was he neglecting the piano?

On September 30, 1925, Ansel wrote to Virginia about his music: "Some day I shall be an *artist,*" but not without six to ten more years of training. Ansel felt he had a duty to his parents and to his talent to commit himself completely to music. He bought a grand piano (with borrowed money) and stopped teaching (it interfered with practicing). "I dedicate my life to my Art," he told Virginia. Though he still loved her, marriage would take too much time and money. Ansel sadly broke their engagement.

Lonely, he went to more parties at Cedric Wright's. Cedric asked Ansel to bring some of his prints along one evening. After a steaming spaghetti dinner, Cedric introduced Ansel to Albert Bender, a wealthy art lover. Albert liked Ansel's soft, shimmering prints so much that he offered to sponsor publication of a small collection. Ansel was ecstatic. The only problem was the title. Albert's publisher refused to have the word *photographs* in it. She said no one would buy an art book of photographs.

After much thinking, they made up the term "parmelian prints" for Ansel's pictures and called the book *Parmelian Prints of the High Sierras.*

Ansel still had doubts about his ability as a photographer. He couldn't express his feelings in photographs as well as he could in music. But he kept trying. And he started seeing Virginia again. They still could not afford to marry, but both were overjoyed to renew their romance.

In April 1927, Ansel joined Virginia and Cedric on a Yosemite hike. They climbed along a rock cleft toward the Diving Board, a granite shelf four thousand feet above the valley floor. Ansel carried twelve heavy glass photo plates to use along the way.

Standing at last in cold wind at the Diving Board, he had only one plate left. Before him loomed the awesome face of Half Dome. Ansel saw in his mind the powerful photograph he wanted, with a deep gray sky and shadowy rocks. He carefully calculated the exposure and filter he needed, and then he snapped the picture. This sharp, intense portrait of the cliff was unlike any of his delicate pictorial prints. *Monolith, The Face of Half Dome* proved to Ansel that photographs could express his strongest emotions.

Ansel began to feel torn between a career in music

and one in photography. Musicians praised his melodious touch on the piano, but he now had money in the bank for the first time—from sales of *Parmelian Prints*. The money did make one choice easier—he could afford to marry Virginia after all.

He rushed to Yosemite to propose. Three days later, on January 2, 1928, they were married in Best's Studio. The couple decided to live with Ansel's parents in the winter and in the valley during summer.

More success with the camera added to Ansel and Virginia's happiness, and by 1930 photography was taking much of Ansel's time and energy. He must choose, he realized, between the camera and the piano.

On one picture-taking trip, he met photographer Paul Strand. Paul belonged to a famous group of New York artists, led by Alfred Stieglitz, who rejected the soft pictorial style of photography. They believed that photographs should be strong and realistic. Paul invited Ansel to look at some of his negatives.

"They were glorious," Ansel later remembered. The simple, sharp images had as much force as a piano concerto. Ansel decided that day—the camera, not the piano, was his future.

③

The Range of Light

The sound of clanking pots pulled the weary hikers up the last yards of rocky trail. Almost two hundred Sierra Club members arrived at the high-country camp, happy to drop their knapsacks while the club's cook served up a hearty dinner. Chewing hot meatballs and gulping black coffee, they rested their blistered feet, swatted mosquitoes, and watched the sun set behind the Sierra. But twenty-nine-year-old Ansel was still out on the trail—sunset is one of the best times for making photographs. By the time the hungry photographer reached camp, there were only cold snacks left to eat.

The annual High Trips were part of the Sierra Club's program to help people know and love the mountains. The month-long adventures grew in popularity every year, as city people tried to spend more time outdoors. The trips were also important for training new club leaders. In the early 1930s, one of the most promising young leaders was the club's black-bearded assistant outings manager and official photographer—Ansel Adams.

With Ansel's guidance, the 1931 High Trip hikers climbed out of Yosemite Valley, over mountain passes, across high meadows, and through thunderstorms to back-country campsites supplied by fifty pack mules. After full days of trekking past lakes and over peaks, the travelers would relax around campfires, singing, making music (some hikers packed violins), or watching plays (Ansel loved to write and star in goofy skits). Sometimes they sat silently, listening to the distant howls of coyotes.

Some nights, club members talked solemnly about conservation problems. One member might mention the miners, foresters, ranchers, or dam builders who were threatening the Sierra. Another would warn that more buildings, roads, and people were crowding Yosemite Valley each year. All agreed that America needed to save more land in national parks.

To help the Sierra Club, Ansel sold photographs to club members, published pictures in the *Sierra Club Bulletin,* and volunteered occasionally at the club's San Francisco office. But Ansel had little time for other club work. Committed to a career in photography, he had to earn a living with his camera. People refused to pay much for artistic photographs. So Ansel, like other artistic photographers, took pictures for advertisements.

He and Virginia built a photographic studio in their new house, which was next door to his parents in San Francisco. Inside, he shot photos of pajamas, glasses, raisin bread, and other products for catalogs and magazines. The advertising jobs were often frustrating because they took time away from his artistic work. But Ansel looked at each assignment as a way to learn more about photography.

His best customer did not want studio pictures anyway. The Yosemite Park and Curry Company wanted to encourage more tourists to visit the valley, especially in winter. When the first all-weather road was built, the company opened a ski area and organized skating, sleighing, and other winter sports. To advertise these attractions, Ansel was hired to take pictures of the new activities and the fancy restaurant in the Ahwahnee Hotel.

Most of his artistic work, though, was back in San Francisco. He wandered near his home, making close-ups of leaves, tree stumps, and old wooden boards. Through these pictures, he expressed his love of small, everyday details of nature.

The sharp photos also showed his rejection of the old fuzzy pictorial style. At a party for artists, Ansel talked about his efforts to make photographs that looked like photographs, not like drawings or paintings. He was delighted to meet several other photographers who shared his goal. Ansel and six other men and women soon decided to form their own group, dedicated to realistic photography. They called themselves "Group f.64," after the tiny lens opening, known as f.64, which photographers used to get sharply focused images.

In November 1932, Group f.64 had their first exhibit of eighty black-and-white prints at the de Young Memorial Museum in San Francisco. Fans of the old style complained, but many critics praised the bold new way of seeing.

The success cheered Ansel, but he still worried that artists outside California might not like his work. What would Alfred Stieglitz, the father of modern photography, have to say? Ansel longed to show his prints to Stieglitz, who ran a famous art gallery in New York City. Like many people, though, Ansel was struggling harder than ever to make a living. Businesses and banks were closing, and thousands of people were losing jobs. Californians had begun to suffer from a national crisis later called the Great Depression. Ansel could barely pay his bills. How could he think of visiting New York?

Happily for Ansel, Virginia's father surprised the couple with enough money for the trip. The train pulled into New York on a rainy morning in March 1933. With a portfolio of prints tucked under one arm, Ansel strode through gray streets past lines of unemployed people waiting for bread. At 509 Madison Avenue, Ansel nervously rode the elevator up to the seventeenth floor and stepped, at last, into a window-lined gallery called An American Place.

Frail, white-haired Alfred Stieglitz glared at the broad-shouldered young mountain climber. Frowning, he agreed to look at the prints. While Stieglitz carefully studied each picture, Ansel perched on the steam radiator, the only spot to sit. Ansel's heart pounded harder and harder as the radiator became hotter and hotter. Finally, Ansel leaped up, and Stieglitz closed the portfolio. The pictures were strong, he told Ansel with a smile. "You are always welcome here."

The meeting with Stieglitz inspired Ansel to open his own gallery, like An American Place, to promote creative photography in California. He worked feverishly to organize his first show, a new exhibit by Group f.64.

Before the gallery opened, he helped lead a Sierra Club trip to Kings Canyon. Virginia, who usually went along, stayed in Yosemite at her father's studio because she was expecting their first child. Concerned about his wife, Ansel hiked home a day early. There, in a Yosemite Valley hospital, the happy father met his new son, Michael.

When the Ansel Adams Gallery opened a month later, hundreds came to see the exhibits. Crowds also visited later shows of paintings, sculptures, and Ansel's own photographs. But Ansel needed to sell the art to earn money, and few visitors could afford to buy during the depression. To support the gallery and his family, he gave lectures, taught workshops, and wrote articles for *Camera Craft* magazine. But the gallery kept losing money. In January 1934, Ansel was forced to give it up.

Disappointed, he spent more time writing, turning his articles into a book. *Making a Photograph* was a hit with amateur photographers, who appreciated Ansel's advice.

Even more exciting, Alfred Stieglitz had asked Ansel to send him some of his best prints. Alfred was preparing the first solo exhibit of Ansel Adams photographs at An American Place.

Without the gallery to run, Ansel also had more time for Sierra Club work. Elected to the club's board of directors in 1934, Ansel became a leader in the campaign to protect the Kings Canyon region of the Sierra. He called the canyon "some of the most rugged and beautiful country in America." But every year, more people demanded that a dam be built on the Kings River to flood part of the canyon. Residents of Los Angeles wanted electricity from the dam, and farmers in the San Joaquin Valley wanted the water to irrigate their crops.

Ansel and the Sierra Club argued that the canyon lands should be saved as a park—but not a resort park like Yosemite, with hotels and parking lots. They wanted an unspoiled landscape, like the few wilderness areas protected in the national forests. No roads should mar the canyon, and only primitive campgrounds should be built for visitors. Then tourists would find not just beautiful scenery but a true wilderness experience.

Since Ansel had often explored and photographed Kings Canyon, the club decided to send him to

Washington, D.C., in 1936 to push Congress to create the first wilderness park. Ansel pounded up and down the halls of the Capitol, knocking on the doors of senators and representatives. Each politician was shown a collection of his Kings Canyon photographs. The beauty of this wilderness, Ansel told them, is threatened by the demands of a few groups. Yet the land's wonders belong to all Americans, now and in the future.

Many officials who met Ansel admired his pictures but still would not vote for the park. Optimistic as usual, Ansel assured other club members that they would just have to keep on fighting.

Ansel's travels often kept him away from San Francisco and his family (which now included two-year-old Anne). When Virginia inherited Best's Studio after her father's death in 1936, she and Ansel decided to move to Yosemite and run the business.

The Adams children went to school in the valley, looking out their classroom windows at passing deer. In the summer, Michael and Anne picnicked in the meadows, waded in the Merced River, and, as they got older, camped with their dad in the mountains. Virginia wrote about the family's happy life in a children's book (illustrated with Ansel's pictures) called *Michael and Anne in Yosemite Valley.*

Living in Yosemite, Ansel could now take mountain photographs in the morning and develop them in the afternoon. A new Sierra Club friend, David Brower, often dropped by the darkroom. While Ansel showed David printing techniques, the pair talked about conservation. And when David stayed late for parties, he loved listening to Ansel play his grand piano. When Ansel played, David later said, you were almost sorry he had chosen the camera over the piano.

Ansel soon found himself working on a new book. The father of a young mountain climber who had died in a fall had asked Ansel to create a book about the Sierra in memory of his son. The Sierra Nevada, called the "Range of Light" by John Muir, had inspired many of Ansel's finest photographs. Through this new book, Ansel hoped to help other people feel the special force and majesty of the California mountains.

In November 1938, Ansel's book *Sierra Nevada: The John Muir Trail* was published. He shipped a copy of the heavy, white book to Alfred Stieglitz. Now a close friend, Alfred wrote back, "You have literally taken my breath away." Another artist and friend wrote, "Your book is like a trip in the High Country again."

Since the book was rich with pictures of Kings Canyon, Ansel thought it could be used in the park campaign. He sent a copy to the highest government official responsible for national parks, Secretary of the Interior Harold Ickes. Secretary Ickes was so moved by the pictures that he gave the book to President Franklin Roosevelt. Already park supporters, both men lobbied Congress to save the area. Ansel and other Sierra Club leaders renewed their fight, publishing newspaper articles and making a film in support of the park. At last, in 1940, Congress voted to create Kings Canyon National Park.

Overjoyed, Ansel was proud of his role in establishing the first wilderness national park. The director of the National Park Service congratulated him on *Sierra Nevada,* saying, "So long as that book is in existence, it will go on justifying the park."

Beautiful beyond Words

The fall of 1940 found Ansel far from his beloved Sierra. His first weeks in New York City were jam-packed with excitement. A friend, Beaumont Newhall, was head of the photograph library at New York's Museum of Modern Art. Together, he and Ansel were creating the first Department of Photography at a major art museum. The department, they believed, would finally give the public a place to discover the finest in creative photography.

Some critics attacked their project, saying that gallery space (and museum money) should be saved for paintings and other "real" art. The two men knew this exhibit must prove that photographs belong in an art museum. They pored over the seven hundred prints in the museum's collection, arguing about which were the best. At last, they chose sixty prints showing photography since the 1840s. Included were pictures by old masters, such as Alfred Stieglitz, and young masters, such as Ansel Adams.

Their exhibit opened on December 31, but Ansel was not there to see its success. Restless in the city and missing Yosemite, he had already caught a train back to California.

Yet he couldn't stay home for very long. His fame as a photographer had won him a teaching position at the Art Center School in Los Angeles. Begin by seeing the picture you want in your head, Ansel advised his students. Then, if your skills are good, the camera can make the photograph that you imagine.

Nearly forty years old, Ansel loved being around younger photographers. And his students loved his warm laugh and generous encouragement. Ansel had discovered a gift for teaching.

To support his family (including his aging parents), he still took professional photography assignments. One day, a letter arrived with the assignment of a lifetime. Secretary of the Interior Harold Ickes, who had admired *Sierra Nevada,* wanted Ansel to travel throughout the country, photographing the national parks and monuments. The pictures would be enlarged into murals to decorate the halls of the Interior Department. The huge job would keep him busy for years. Ansel could hardly believe his good luck.

Ansel's old friend Cedric Wright and eight-year-old son, Michael, eagerly joined him on the first park trip. They all squeezed into a station wagon crammed with 1,500 pounds of cameras, lenses, light meters, film cases, sleeping bags, water jugs, snacks, and extra gasoline. The travelers bounced down rutted roads, through torrential rains, across deserts, and past cactuses, aspen trees, and elk herds. California's Death Valley, Arizona's Grand Canyon, and Utah's Zion were some of the first parks they explored.

Camping under the stars every night, Ansel woke in the darkness before dawn to fry breakfast steaks and set up his cameras. Michael handed film and lenses up to his father, who worked on a wooden camera platform on the car roof. As sunrise approached, each held his breath. Would the wind jiggle the camera? Would the clouds, light, and shadows be right? Only if the scene was as grand as Ansel imagined would he release the shutter.

Ansel returned home with splendid images of rolling sand dunes, wind-sculpted cliffs, and billowing thunderclouds. Each picture captured Ansel's feelings of awe and respect toward nature. These photographs showed a confident, dramatic artistry. Some were masterpieces.

Many people, however, criticized Ansel's work. During the depression, many photographers (even a few from Group f.64) turned away from artistic photography. With so many Americans unemployed, poor, and hungry, critics thought that photographers should focus on society's problems. Ansel's friend Dorothea Lange and others had begun using their cameras to document human suffering—in the hope that people shocked by the pictures would seek solutions.

In the late 1930s, documentary photographs of battlefields and bombed cities stirred fear and anger in Americans as the Nazis dragged Europe into war. The world is falling to pieces, one critic railed, and Ansel Adams is photographing rocks!

Ansel, too, was sickened by the poverty, destruction, and bloodshed. But he argued that humans always need the inspiration of art, especially in their darkest hours. And natural beauty, he believed, would last to inspire people long after the war. He vowed to keep working on the park project even after the United States entered World War II.

Ansel could not keep that promise to himself. As the fighting intensified, the U.S. government concentrated more resources on the war effort. Even Yosemite's Ahwahnee Hotel was converted into a military hospital. Plans for the park murals were canceled.

Though sorely disappointed, Ansel knew that all Americans must make sacrifices to overcome the crisis. What could he do to help? Beaumont Newhall had signed up as a lieutenant in the Army Air Forces. Sierra Club outings and much conservation work came to a halt because one-fourth of the club's members were now in uniform. Ansel tried to enlist, but as a forty-year-old with small children, he was rejected. Instead, the government asked him to develop top-secret photographs, train army photographers, and lead troops on practice patrols through Yosemite. He later said, "I volunteered for any war-related job I could find." But he wanted to do more.

As the war dragged on, Ansel's frustration grew. He talked about it one day to a Sierra Club friend, Ralph Merritt, who was visiting Yosemite. Ralph was the new director of the Manzanar War Relocation Center, one of ten prison camps holding Japanese Americans during World War II. Enraged by Japan's attack on Pearl Harbor, many Americans blamed all Japanese people. Japanese immigrants and their American-born children were suspected of being spies for the enemy.

On February 19, 1942, President Roosevelt had signed Executive Order 9066, forcing more than 100,000 people with Japanese ancestry into relocation camps. Torn from their homes and jobs, they were suddenly surrounded by barbed wire and armed guards in isolated parts of the West.

Though head of the Manzanar camp, Ralph opposed locking up innocent citizens. Ansel shared his outrage. Ralph couldn't pay Ansel, but he believed there should be a photographic record of this tragic mistake. Ansel later said, "I immediately accepted the challenge."

The Manzanar camp lay in dry Owens Valley, between the Sierra Nevada range to the west and the White Mountains to the east. Families were crowded into crude, tar-paper barracks, where they slept on cots under army blankets. In summer, temperatures rose to 110° F, and the wind whipped desert dust through cracks in the walls.

Yet the people Ansel saw in the camp were not overwhelmed by bitterness. They were running small stores, publishing a newspaper, and growing their own food. Along the camp's only creek, they had built a tiny, shaded park. Their dignity and hopefulness touched Ansel deeply. With his camera, he documented Manzanar's daily life.

Pictures of farmers planting potatoes, students writing, and families gathering for church were all evidence of the prisoners' great courage. Ansel believed the majestic mountains surrounding Manzanar helped lift their spirits in the face of injustice.

A book of these photographs, *Born Free and Equal,* was published in 1944. People who feared Japanese Americans called it "disloyal." Some parents whose sons had died in battle wrote Ansel furious letters, and copies of the book were publicly burned. Although pained by such reactions, Ansel remained proud of his book. The camps, however, were not closed until the war ended in 1945.

When soldiers returned from the war, many families built new houses, bought new cars, and went on vacations. More forests than ever were being cut down for lumber and more rivers dammed for electricity. The national parks were overrun with people escaping from the bustling cities. And when they reached the parks, the tourists expected restaurants, bars, bowling alleys, pools, and plenty of parking to make their trips comfortable and exciting.

Ansel and other conservationists feared that the parks would be damaged forever by too much use —"loved to death." Ansel now regretted the advertising photographs he had made. To make matters worse, a new park rule forced him to close his Yosemite photography business. Although Virginia still owned Best's Studio, the family moved back to San Francisco.

Ansel longed to share his strong feelings about parks. In 1946 he won a Guggenheim Fellowship, a grant that would pay him once again to photograph national parks across the country.

By car and by train, he explored Carlsbad Caverns in New Mexico, Big Bend in Texas, and Mount Rainier in Washington. A steamship carried him to photograph volcanoes in the Territory of Hawaii. Another ship took Ansel and his fourteen-year-old son to Juneau, capital of the Alaska Territory. There, at the edge of the great wilderness, Ansel faced an obstacle. The only way to travel was by plane—but Ansel was terrified of flying! It didn't help that the tiny seaplane he and Michael were to board was called *The Flying Coffin*.

Michael whooped with excitement each time the plane zoomed over a mountain or swooped into a valley. As blue-white glaciers, evergreen forests, and galloping moose slipped beneath them, a feeling of wonder replaced Ansel's fears. He wrote to friends, "I am afraid Alaska is the place for me. I am NUTS about it."

The trip to Alaska, and another in 1948, were turning points for Ansel. He said, "In Alaska I felt the full force of vast space and wildness." Popular parks like Yosemite seemed cramped and tame in comparison. He realized that only a century ago, the Sierra had also been a huge wilderness. But logging, ranching, dams, and roads had carved it into smaller and smaller pieces. The parks remaining were being turned into overcrowded playgrounds. Soon there would be nowhere left to experience nature in its wild state.

How could this destruction be stopped? People still saw land, Ansel believed, as merely a source for making money from lumber or minerals. Or they saw fortunes to be made from millions of tourists. They did not see nature as a priceless source of spiritual and artistic inspiration the way he did.

John Muir had once changed people's attitudes toward Yosemite through his writings. Ansel Adams now vowed to change the public's values with his camera—to inspire a love of wild lands through images more beautiful than words.

⑤

The American Earth

Ansel slowly turned the pages of his new book, *My Camera in the National Parks.* His photographs of Alaska's Glacier Bay and the other parks he had visited were perfectly reproduced, as he required them to be in all his books. The new book was selling well. But Ansel still felt frustrated. As with his other books, most people who bought it were Sierra Club members and others who already loved wild places. How could he reach the people he wanted most to reach—the people who didn't care?

Ansel was too busy to answer that question. Nearly fifty years old, he was teaching photography at the California School of Fine Arts and writing a series of photography textbooks. Also, a friend named Edwin Land had recently invented a kind of "instant" photography, and Ansel was testing Land's new Polaroid cameras.

He was also experimenting with color photography. Black-and-white photographs had more artistic power, Ansel thought, but color photography was a new challenge. He especially liked making Colorama murals of meadows, farms, and other landscapes for the Kodak Company to hang in New York City's Grand Central Station. Each Colorama was eighteen feet high and sixty feet long, and had to be rolled up like a rug to ship to the station.

Family troubles kept Ansel occupied too. After years of poor health, his mother died in 1950. A second blow fell the next year when Charles Adams died. Never would Ansel forget Charles's kindness and love of nature.

Ansel's friend Beaumont Newhall and his wife, Nancy, had moved to Rochester, New York, where Beaumont was manager of the George Eastman House. Nancy was a respected writer and designer of photography exhibits. She worked with Ansel on several articles and books on the western United States. Ansel made the pictures and Nancy provided the words.

In 1954 Ansel asked Nancy to help with another task—teaching Yosemite visitors about protecting nature. For the Sierra Club's LeConte Lodge, Ansel envisioned a photography exhibit showing how the land is damaged when people cut trees, graze sheep, or dig mines. And it would show the wild park lands still remaining. Viewers, he believed, would then understand how land has spiritual worth more valuable than money. Nancy researched the subject in Rochester and wrote a long poem for the text.

After months of work, she and Ansel met in San Francisco to select photographs to tell the story. They picked 102 images: 54 by Ansel and 48 by other respected photographers, including Edward Weston, Eliot Porter, and Margaret Bourke-White. And they chose an exhibit title: "This Is the American Earth."

Nancy's poetry worked with Ansel's dramatic pictures like lyrics with a tune. Their images of mountains, wildlife, rivers, and people stirred the emotions of Yosemite visitors. David Brower, Ansel's old friend and the Sierra Club's new executive director, said the exhibit was as beautiful as a symphony. So successful was the exhibit that it was sent around the country by the Smithsonian Institution and throughout Europe by the United States Information Agency.

Ansel wanted to reach still more people. He and Nancy decided to turn the exhibit into a book. Even as they returned to work, tourists were flooding into the national parks, and Ansel was worried.

A new ten-year National Park Service plan called for the building of additional roads, picnic grounds, parking lots, outdoor theaters, ranger stations, and bathrooms—all to invite more tourists.

At Yosemite, the National Park Service was planning to widen and straighten an old mining road so that visitors could speed from the valley into the high country. Ansel had often traveled the narrow, snaking Tioga Road on his trips to Manzanar, and he knew that it passed near the glacier-polished shores of Lake Tenaya. The proposed construction would cut across the granite domes, scarring the mountains forever.

Ansel proposed an alternate route away from the lake and fired off angry telegrams to government officials in Washington, D.C. When a few politicians expressed concern, Ansel guided them to the threatened shore.

Despite his efforts, the bulldozers and blasting crews arrived. Ansel mourned the devastation in a 1958 article for the *Sierra Club Bulletin* called "Tenaya Tragedy." To him, building roads for speed and comfort violated the purpose of national parks. It was a bitter defeat for Ansel. The Tioga Road proved to him again that others did not yet respect the wild land he loved.

Finishing his book with Nancy took on fresh urgency. When they could not find a publisher, the partners worked with David Brower to design a book the Sierra Club could publish itself. *This Is the American Earth,* published in 1960, won applause from artists and preservationists alike. Supreme Court Justice William O. Douglas called it "one of the great statements in the history of conservation." And as Ansel had hoped, it was purchased by tens of thousands of people who knew little about the natural world. Many kept the book on their coffee tables because it was beautiful—and learned more about nature every time they turned its pages.

Just as important, the book launched the Sierra Club's series of "exhibit format" books, each with glorious nature photographs. The books raised money for the club's work and convinced thousands to join the fight to save the land, air, and water.

As public concern for nature grew in the 1960s, a new movement called "environmentalism" was born. This progress thrilled Ansel, as did the other good things happening in his life. Nancy Newhall was designing a huge exhibit of his life's work for the de Young Museum in San Francisco. Photography students flocked to his workshops in Yosemite each summer. And he and Virginia had a new house in Carmel, California, on a hill overlooking the ocean.

Over sixty years old and a grandfather, Ansel had a gray beard, bald head, and deep lines around his eyes when he smiled. It was hard for him to climb mountains to make pictures. But thousands of negatives from years of camera work still needed printing. So, ignoring the pain in his arthritic fingers, he spent hours each day in his darkroom—pausing only to grab snacks in the kitchen. At day's end, he might play his piano or welcome Sierra Club friends who dropped by to watch the sunset through his windows.

As the Sierra Club grew, so did its political strength. In the 1960s, the club successfully pushed for new laws protecting parks and wilderness. But success, in some cases, brought problems. The club pressured the Pacific Gas and Electric Company not to build their planned nuclear power plant in a desert area called the Nipomo Dunes. When the company decided to build instead in Diablo Canyon, Ansel declared a victory. But other club members, including David Brower, objected angrily. The canyon deserves protection too, they stated.

Ansel argued that people need electricity; land use and protection must be balanced. He didn't want the club wasting time on the power plant while acres of wilderness were disappearing. Only after the plant was built and an earthquake faultline was discovered in the canyon did Ansel question his position.

The bitter fight over Diablo Canyon left tension between Ansel and David Brower. Fearing that his old friend was leading the Sierra Club the wrong way, Ansel reluctantly led the campaign to push him out.

But even after David resigned in 1969, Ansel felt out of place on the board of directors. The Sierra Club had grown from a small group protecting California wilderness into a large organization battling national problems such as pesticide use, acid rain, smog, and oil spills. The club needed scientists and lawyers, Ansel thought, not artists. After thirty-seven years on the board, he resigned in 1971.

Leaving the Sierra Club board, Ansel later said, gave him the freedom to accomplish more on his own. Although concerned about all environmental problems, his passion was for wilderness preservation. Despite a painful heart problem, he spoke at conferences and lectures about the importance of saving the last wild places.

Every chance he got, he gave speeches about the need to teach people to love nature. Environmental education is not about teaching dull facts, he said. It is about awakening feelings of awe and mystery toward the natural world. People who learn to care deeply about a park, Ansel said, will not treat it like a playground.

He even took his message to the White House. President Gerald Ford listened to his advice on national park policy. In 1979 Ansel met President Jimmy Carter while making Carter's official portrait. It was the first presidential portrait by a photographer. Ansel and President Carter became friends and allies in the campaign to reserve millions of acres of Alaska as parks and wildlife refuges. A grateful president awarded Ansel the Presidential Medal of Freedom for his lifetime achievements as an artist and environmentalist. But Ansel's greatest reward came on December 2, 1980, when President Carter signed a bill reserving 104 million acres of Alaskan wilderness.

Ansel proudly accepted the many other honors and awards he had earned. The Wilderness Society presented him with the first Ansel Adams Award for Conservation in 1980. The next year, Harvard University awarded him an Honorary Doctor of Fine Arts degree. And one of his prints, *Moonrise, Hernandez, New Mexico,* sold at auction for $71,500 —a record price for a creative photograph.

A weakening heart sapped Ansel's energy as he turned eighty. Sometimes, even short walks left him out of breath. But he still did all in his power to safeguard the wild. As a new president came to the White House, Ansel became horrified at the change in policies toward land, air, and water. President Ronald Reagan wanted to open parks and other public lands to private industry. Ansel feared that mountains would be stripped of timber, parks slashed with roads, and coastlines littered with oil derricks. In furious letters to politicians and newspapers, he attacked the policies as greedy and shortsighted. Though they might make money today, Ansel asserted, such actions would do permanent harm to America's greatest treasures.

He urged younger environmentalists to take action: Write letters, sign petitions, and hold marches. To William Turnage, a close friend and executive director of the Wilderness Society, he wrote, "It is to be the biggest fight we have had. I wish I was fifty years younger!" But as always, eighty-one-year-old Ansel was eager to do whatever he could. Ready for the fight, he signed his letter, "LET'S GO!!!"

Afterword

On April 22, 1984, Ansel's heart failed. He died peacefully in Carmel, California, at age eighty-two. That year, fellow artists celebrated his achievements in an exhibition of his photographs. Two California senators sponsored a bill preserving 100,000 acres of the Sierra Nevada as the Ansel Adams Wilderness. On the first anniversary of his death, friends and fellow environmentalists gathered in Yosemite to name a mountain peak "Mount Ansel Adams."

Ansel's work is carried on by many people. Photographs today are a powerful tool in the environmental movement, inspiring people to save mountains, deserts, beaches, and rain forests. Ansel's own photographs, in books, calendars, and posters, capture the feeling of wildness, even for people in the city. A permanent exhibit can be seen at the Wilderness Society headquarters in Washington, D.C.

The problems Ansel battled are still with us. Ansel wanted his art to move people to experience nature. Take hikes, climb mountains, and explore parks, he prodded. Only when people love and experience wilderness will they fight to save wild places. Only then will nature be treasured in the Kings Canyon Sierra, in Alaska, across America and the earth.

Bibliography

Primary Sources

Adams, Ansel. *Making a Photograph.* London and New York: The Studio Publications, 1935.

———. *My Camera in the National Parks.* Boston: Houghton Mifflin, 1950.

———. *Sierra Nevada: The John Muir Trail.* Berkeley: Archetype Press, 1938.

———. "Tenaya tragedy." *Sierra Club Bulletin* 43 (November 1958): 1-4.

Adams, Ansel, with Mary Street Alinder. *Ansel Adams: An Autobiography.* Boston: Little, Brown and Company, 1985.

Adams, Ansel, and Nancy Newhall. *This Is the American Earth.* San Francisco: Sierra Club, 1960.

Adams, Virginia. *Michael and Anne in Yosemite Valley.* London and New York: The Studio Publications, 1941.

Alinder, Mary, and Andrea Stillman, eds. *Ansel Adams: Letters and Images 1916–1984.* Boston: Little, Brown and Company, 1988.

Siri, William, and Ansel Adams. "Diablo Canyon Again—and Again, and Again." *Sierra Club Bulletin* 54 (February 1969): 4-5.

Secondary Sources

Cohen, Michael. *The History of the Sierra Club: 1892–1970.* San Francisco: Sierra Club Books, 1988.

Haip, Renee. "The Impact of the Photographer on Wilderness Appreciation: A Case Study of Ansel Adams." Master's thesis, University of Arizona, 1990.

Hutchings, James. *In the Heart of the Sierras: Yosemite Valley and the Big Tree Groves.* Lafayette, Calif.: Great West Books, 1990 (1886).

Newhall, Nancy. *Ansel Adams: The Eloquent Light.* San Francisco: Sierra Club, 1963.

Read, Michael, ed. *Ansel Adams: New Light.* San Francisco: Friends of Photography, 1993.

Runte, Alfred. *Yosemite: The Embattled Wilderness.* Lincoln: University of Nebraska Press, 1990.

Turnage, Robert. "Ansel Adams: The Role of the Artist in the Environmental Movement." *The Living Wilderness* 43 (March 1980): 4-13.